WILDLIFE IN BLOOM SERIES

Little Skunk

BY AUTHOR & CONSERVATIONIST

LINDA BLACKMOOR

ISBN: 978-1-966417-00-2 (PRINT)

PUBLISHED BY QUILL PRESS. LINDA BLACKMOOR'S TITLES MAY BE PURCHASED IN BULK FOR EDUCATIONAL, BUSINESS, FUNDRAISING, OR SALES PROMOTIONAL USE. FOR INFORMATION, PLEASE EMAIL HELLO@LINDABLACKMOOR.COM

FIRST PRINT EDITION: 2024

LINDA BLACKMOOR
WWW.LINDABLACKMOOR.COM

SPECIES

Skunks include twelve species like the striped skunk, spotted skunk, and hooded skunk found across the Americas and Southeast Asia. Ranging from the small pygmy spotted skunk to the larger striped skunk, each boasts unique fur patterns and habitats, some even residing in Indonesia and the Philippines. Their diversity reflects incredible adaptability to forests, deserts, mountains, and even neighborhoods.

SKUNK FACT #2

STRIPES

Skunks wear bold black-and-white coats with stripes or spots that serve as natural warning signs to predators. Each species has its own pattern—some display a single stripe, others have multiple stripes or spots like the eastern spotted skunk. These distinctive markings make skunks unmistakable and help them stand out in the animal kingdom.

WINTER

Skunks do not truly hibernate but enter a state called torpor during the cold winter months, becoming less active and staying in their dens for extended periods. They often share dens with other skunks for warmth, sometimes with several females and a male huddling together. During torpor, their metabolism slows down, and they rely on stored body fat to survive when food is scarce.

NIGHT

Skunks are nocturnal, awakening at dusk to begin their nightly explorations using their sharp senses of smell and hearing to find food. They have poor eyesight but rely on their sensitive noses and ears to navigate the darkness. During the day, they rest in burrows or dens to avoid predators and the heat of the sun. This nighttime lifestyle helps them avoid many daytime dangers and reduces competition for food.

SKUNK FACT #5

OMNIVORE

Skunks are omnivores, enjoying a diet of insects, grubs, small rodents, eggs, fruits, berries, nuts, and plants, making them pest controllers. By eating insects like beetles, grasshoppers, and crickets, they help protect crops from damage. They also consume wasps and bees, sometimes digging up nests to eat the larvae inside. Their varied diet allows them to adjust to seasonal changes in food.

DIGGING

With strong front claws, skunks are expert diggers, creating burrows and unearthing insects, grubs, and roots for food. They often craft their own dens or take over abandoned burrows of animals like groundhogs, lining them with leaves and grass for warmth. Their digging helps aerate the soil, promoting healthy plant growth and soil health. Their excavations also help control insect populations.

MUSK

Skunks have special glands that produce a powerful musk, which they can spray accurately up to 10 feet to deter predators. This oily liquid contains sulfur compounds that create a strong, lasting odor detectable by humans up to a mile away. Before spraying, skunks give warning signs like stamping their feet, hissing, and raising their tails to give threats a chance to retreat.

SKUNK FACT #8

PREDATOR

Despite their smelly defense, skunks have predators like great horned owls, which hunt them because they lack a strong sense of smell. Other predators include coyotes, foxes, bobcats, and domestic dogs, especially preying on young or inexperienced skunks. Snakes and birds of prey may also target skunk kits when they are vulnerable. This predator-prey relationship helps maintain balance in the ecosystem.

LIFESPAN

Skunks typically live about 3 years in the wild due to threats like predators, diseases, harsh weather, and vehicle collisions, but can live up to 10 years in captivity with proper care. They reach maturity at about one year old, ready to start families of their own. Their survival depends on their ability to find food, shelter, and avoid dangers in their environment.

SKUNK FACT #10

BURROWS

Skunks use burrows for resting, hiding, and raising their young, often with multiple entrances for quick escapes from predators. They may dig their own dens or use abandoned burrows of other animals, sometimes under buildings or rock piles. Female skunks give birth to litters of 4 to 7 kits in the spring, caring for them in the safety of the burrow until they're ready to explore at two months old.

SKUNK FACT #11

SOUNDS

Skunks communicate using sounds such as chirps, squeals, hisses, growls, and grunts, along with body language like tail movements and stamping feet. They also use scent marking by secreting small amounts of musk to establish territory or attract mates. These signals help them express fear, aggression, or readiness to mate, and to keep other skunks away from their dens.

RABIES

Skunks can carry rabies, a disease that affects the nervous system and can be transmitted to humans and pets through bites. This makes them one of the most common carriers of rabies in some regions, along with raccoons and bats. Rabies can cause animals to behave unusually, sometimes making them more aggressive or disoriented. Staying informed around wild skunks keeps people and animals safe.

ADAPT

Skunks demonstrate incredible adaptability, thriving in habitats ranging from woodlands and grasslands to deserts and urban areas. They often live near humans, finding shelter under porches, sheds, or in abandoned buildings, and scavenging for food in gardens, compost piles, or trash cans. This ability to exploit various food sources and shelters allows them to survive in changing environments.

www.ingramcontent.com/pod-product-compliance
Lightning Source LLC
Chambersburg PA
CBHW060838270326
41933CB00002B/122

9781966417002